GO ALL IN

A FORMULA TO ACCELERATE YOUR SUCCESS

BY NIM STANT

What You Seek Is Seeking You.
-Rumi

Go All In

Copyright © 2020 by Nim Stant

All rights reserved.

Permission to reproduce or transmit in any form or by any means, electronic or mechanical, including photocopying, photographic and recording audio or video, or by any information storage and retrieval system, must be obtained in writing from the author.

Go All In is a registered trademark of Nim Stant.

To order additional copies of this title, e-mail:

_____

The author may be contacted at the following e-mail address:

nimstant@gmail.com
website: nimstant.com

First printing November 2020

Library of Congress Cataloging-in-Publication Data

> Stant, Nim
> Go all in : a formula to accelerate your success / by Nim Stant
> p. cm
> ISBN: 9798620713233
> 1. Success. 2. Self help. 3. Mindset.
> 4. Goal setting. 5. Coaching. 6. High performance.
> 7. Habits.

Printed in the U.S.A.

14 13 12 11 10   1 2 3 4 5 6 7 8 9 10

Dedicated to my children, Sam and Sariah, who consistently inspire me to keep going all in throughout my life. You help me become a better person everyday and help me fulfill my mission.

CONTENTS

INTRODUCTION... 7

BEYOND THE COMFORT ZONE: The Quest For Quantum Success... 21

SECTION ONE: Decisions are Everything................ 32
1 There is No Shortage of Success......................... 39
2 Be Uncomfortable.. 44
3 Commit First, Figure Out Later............................. 58

SECTION TWO: Get Super Clear 69
4 The Power of Goals.. 74
5 You Have to Give Up to Grow Up......................... 84
6 Empowerment from the Inside Out....................... 89

SECTION THREE: Finding Mentors........................ 100
7 Asking for Help... 108
8 If You Want to Be a Millionaire, Talk With a Billionaire... 113
9 What to Look for in a Mentor................................ 123

SECTION FOUR: Go "All In" and Overcommit......... 127
10 Overcoming Time Wasters.................................. 134
11 Expand. Never Contract..................................... 140
12 Getting Started with Go All In............................. 146

About the Author... 163

INTRODUCTION

We can all achieve and enjoy long-term success, but we must search out and vigorously employ new behaviors, new attitudes, and be willing to break out of our routines in order to go all the way in and create quantum success.

What You Seek Is Seeking You.
Whatever You're Looking For Can Only Be Found Inside of You.

—Rumi

Have you ever wondered?

How do highly successful people, professional dancers, and athletes achieve their goals? What do they know about what it takes to succeed? Why do they routinely go far beyond what most people would do to win? Why do they spend eight hours a day practicing the same move over and over again?

The amateur practices until they get it right, but the professional practices until they don't get it wrong anymore! It takes pushing the body to its limits to understand that the only real limitation is in the mind. It takes repeating the same move over and over and over again to perfect that move or to get it precisely how you want it. Andre Agassi said he had to hit tennis balls 6,000 times per day to get it right. He practiced on the tennis court in their backyard.

While training as a professional dancer, I would practice spinning on my heels 100 times a day just to get to the right spot and the right focus. I kept doing it until the skin came off my heels and the doctor told me to rest for two weeks to let it heal. I didn't stop and rest. I kept practicing — despite my injury and the doctor's advice — to get my moves right.

It's the same whether you want to build a six or seven-figure company, or lose weight, or become an expert in cooking. You will need resilience to face the fear of failing over and over again because it will keep popping up. It takes facing your deepest fears to conquer them. It takes falling over a hundred times and getting back up a thousand more to win.

And while the journey may be long, the toughest challenges will bring the greatest rewards. Highly successful people know that overcoming the doubts in their mind leaves a heart full of faith.

We must embrace truth, compassion, and tolerance. To change the world, we must work on ourselves first.

Sharing this message and inspiring others is part of the legacy I intend to leave — that is my long term life goal. When I die, I want my children to remember me and my message of *never giving up* — so I have to change myself and work hard on myself first. I need to keep improving so others will continue to believe in me and feel impacted by my work. My efforts will affect them and improve the world. Understand that "the world" doesn't have to mean billions of people. It can just be a few people whose lives you've changed.

We all have goals. Big or small, it doesn't matter. Some people want to be good at baking because baking cakes make people happy, and that's a great goal. It doesn't have to be a goal on Oprah's level. Homeschooling your kids might be your world, and that's fantastic, but you have to decide what you want and educate yourself first. No matter what it takes, it's worth it.

When you picked up this book, you may have thought, "What does 'Go All In' mean exactly and how will it help me?" Something pulled you to find out more about how to achieve your goals. You're ready and you want to learn the best way to invest your time and energy to get the best results possible.

Most of us have been taught by society to "play it safe" or to "take it slow". Most of us live our daily lives in agreement with the notion that we shouldn't go for the big risks because we don't want to end up failing. I used to think like that too! However, this mentality is totally the opposite of the "Go All In" principle.

I used to play it safe in every area of my life thinking that it was the way to create a solid, fulfilling life; but that way of thinking didn't translate to fulfillment. It didn't take me to where I wanted to go, and I wasn't the person I wanted to be either. I was pretending by not saying what I'd really thought. At my business, I wouldn't look at my numbers. I didn't want to see how much I'd spent, or exactly how much I was making each month. I wasn't ready to commit to my success at that time. So I told myself, "That's it! I'm done with being scared and staying behind this curtain. I am ready to leave the mask behind and go all in to improve every area of my life and if I fail, I will fail very fast, and learn quickly that it was not the right way to go."

I was a kid from the third world country of Thailand. Thirty years ago, when I told people I was from Thailand, most of them had no idea where Thailand was on the map. This made me feel small and unimportant. I didn't grow up in the kind of family that has a parent planning my career success. I didn't go to the best school. I didn't have connections to get work or have anyone who invested in me. I didn't have that kind of "get rich quick" luck. In fact, there was no luck at all in my life. I have created all my success by myself because I invested in myself. I went out of my way to connect with people I admired. I believe that I have been able to get to where I am today because I had invested in my life and studied "the mechanics of success" for the last two decades.

So, what does "Go All In" really mean? Going all in is overcommitting to achieving your goals. That means setting the intention knowing that you'll meet it. Going all in requires a full commitment to what you want because the success you are looking for will be the result of this level of commitment.

As I look back over my life, I see that the one thing that was consistent with any success I've ever achieved was that I always went all in and put 100% of my energy into the project. I committed fully, regularly offering ten times more input and activity than others did. However, let me be very clear here. I do not think that I've created an extraordinary level of success. I am completely aware that there are a lot of people who are many times more successful than I am. However, I have created my successful retreat business from scratch and that has allowed me to enjoy a wonderful lifestyle that is perfect for me.

As I talk about going all in for success throughout this book, I definitely mean any kind of success. Yes, you can create any kind of success for yourself. It all requires the same action steps to "Go All In". It doesn't matter if you want to start a new business, lose weight, get a dysfunctional relationship back on track, travel the world, free yourself of an addiction, or any other goal. They all require you to commit fully to your goal.

This "Go All In" principle isn't about special gifts, talents, luck, or skill. It is the decision and the commitment to put forth all you have to the vision of where you want to be — that big picture you're envisioning for yourself or your family.

The wonderful reality is that when you go all in, you will see that it is in fact an easier step to take than doing 50/50 and playing it safe! I always tell my coaching clients that since you gotta work hard for your dreams anyway, why don't you dream big — as big as you want — and commit to take action and work hard, giving it your 100%? You will see the real results faster or bigger if you really go full-out. When you go all the way in and put all your focus toward your goal, you are on your way to achieving your goals and the success you've been dreaming of.

So in this book, *Go All In*, I want to show you the formula to accelerate your success. You can dream as big as you want, give it the best you've got, and build your own success. I will teach you how you can make the right decision for the next right move for you — the one that will get you to where you want to be.

If you are an entrepreneur just like me, you will find that the formula I'm sharing in this book is insanely effective. You can use every single step I share to reach your goals. If you are someone who is looking for better health, you will find that changing your mindset will totally impact the outcome too. If you are a parent, this is a good book to help you teach and train your children that persistence and commitment are the keys to having a fulfilling and accomplished life. Learning to go all in and to never give up helps children become self-reliant and confident as they discover that they can create exactly the kind of life they want for themselves.

I hope that this book will impact you and inspire you to be who you love to be, do what you dream to do, and appreciate your life every day. My heart goes out to you. I'm cheering for you and would love to hear more about your success.

Remember, success is not an accident. It's the decision to take full action, commit, and go all the way in!

My mom, my sister (right), and me (left).

Go All In

"Anyone that suggests to me to do less is either not a real friend or very confused!"

- Grant Cardone,
The 10X Rule: The Only Difference Between Success and Failure

BEYOND THE COMFORT ZONE:
The Quest For Quantum Success

Don't be surprised if you feel uneasy. It's part of the process.

Committing to your goal and using this go all in formula will jerk you out of your comfort zone. It will make you uneasy. That's a good sign, so press on.

I didn't want to wake up and face reality!

2020 was supposed to be an amazing year for many of us — including myself. However, the world suddenly became filled with so much trouble. More and more people were getting sick and dying from the coronavirus and it quickly became a world pandemic. My yoga retreat business came to a screeching halt. It was devastating, but I had no choice but to postpone the upcoming retreats and look for another way to serve my clients.

When the year started, I never imagined that the struggles would show up as they did. The world pandemic forced me to stop my yoga retreat business, and subsequently, most of my clients canceled their bookings with me. I had to refund tens of thousands of dollars while figuring out my next move. It wasn't a fun moment at all. I was super stressed and felt absolutely hopeless. I didn't know where to go and what to do. What was the next right thing? For once in my life, I had no idea. That's the only thing I could honestly answer at that moment: I didn't know what my next move would be.

I allowed myself to stress and stay in this darkness for three days, and then I told myself, "I'm NOT letting this stop me! I'll gather all the energy I have left and get back up. I'll grab a blank sheet of paper and start brainstorming ideas about how I could make money and start pivoting my business!" Within that same week, I created a new homepage for my website, changed all my strategies, and started promoting and marketing my business. Then Kajabi, one of the most powerful online teaching platforms, started to notice the changes I made in my business and contacted me, asking if they could interview me right away. They published that interview on their website soon after. About 47,000 entrepreneurs were inspired by the article and how I made the right move to pivot my business and they began to do the same.

People have asked me how and why I decided to expand my business — and my entire perspective on life — exactly at the time when things were most uncertain. They wondered why I would take risks at a time when the economy was slipping into a recession. The truth is, I would rather die expanding and doing what I love than live in contraction — wasting my breath each day. I would rather fail pushing forward than stay in the same place, playing it safe, watching, and repeating what everyone else does. This, quite frankly, would kill me too quickly and too soon.

I remember, years ago while growing up in Thailand, I had landed a really well-paying job working for a jewelry company in customer service. I was only twenty-two but because I spoke English, they paid me ten times what they paid than other Thais. My job was to answer emails from our customers around the world and help them with any problems or concerns they might have with our products. I sat in front of the computer all day. However, I couldn't stand it for more than four days before I ran away. I quit the job within four days because it didn't feed my purpose. Since then, I've known that I will never waste my time doing things that don't serve my life goals.

I am sharing this with you because I want to show you the power of "Going All In". You become unstoppable as soon as you make the decision to commit 100% to whatever you want to achieve. The obstacles you face aren't there to make you suffer. Those obstacles are really a detour to take you in the right direction.

I am thankful that I listened to myself at that time and said "no" to a trap that would have kept me from where I am today. If I hadn't, I wouldn't be living my purpose every day, accompanied by my beautiful, loving family. I wouldn't be running my business from home while raising my wonderful children.

I am so glad I didn't "play it safe" just to say I had a job. Because I went all in, I am able to serve my community, lead international yoga retreats, and make money while hanging out on the beach and having fun with my amazing clients.

Life is so much better than it would have been because I decided to make it wonderful. You can create your life this way too. I invite you to stop playing it safe and go all in for your dreams. You'll be so glad that you did.

Twenty years ago, most people viewed career success differently than they do nowadays. Most people were convinced that going to college, getting a degree, finding a full-time job, and having a fixed salary was the safest way to go considering the economy. Well, if you allow the economy to determine your choices, you'll never be in control of your own economy. Your energy, personality, and creativity are worth more than just living day by day doing what you don't enjoy but think you have to do. Go all in and put your energy towards where you'd love to be even though it makes you feel super uncomfortable doing that. If you want to expand to success, you need to get attention by taking massive action.

Going all in means you need to burn the place down, keep adding wood to your fire until you succeed in becoming what you want to be. Don't wait. Don't stop. Ever! Keep stacking the wood until the fire in you is so hot that you can't just sit on your sofa at your home. You'll have to get out and do something new that will give you the results you want to see.

If you want to lose weight and get back to a healthy body, you need to keep adding the wood to your inner fire, so it burns and pushes you to get out, exercise, eat differently, and seek all the help you need to succeed. You need to burn the place down until you triumph. When you begin to heat things up, you will start to be aware that what you have done before isn't enough.

Obsession isn't a disease — it's a gift! If you want to start a new level of success, you need to be a little obsessed with taking massive actions towards any possibility that will take you to your results. Once you get going, keep going. Continue taking action until you can't stop your forward momentum. This is the key! You must keep the forward momentum going.

It's just like how you learned to ride a bike as a little kid — you first started with the training wheels. Once you could do that, then your parents took off the training wheels. When they did, you surely, suddenly lost confidence and were scared of falling. You were afraid to get hurt, but your parents wanted you to learn, so you tried riding without the training wheels. You fell sometimes, and you rode sometimes. You stopped, rested, and kept going. Little by little, you improved. You started to get used to the feel of it, and finally, you just took off. You did it! You could finally ride the bike without the training wheels and your parents' help.

That's the forward momentum I am talking about. You keep going, taking action, and going some more until you get it.

Success tends to bless those who are most committed to giving it the attention it deserves. So keep going all in and taking massive actions. Don't ever settle for taking an average amount of action or only going in 50%. The things that matter to you are worth all you've got.

This book is designed to help you take clear steps and laser focus on the action steps needed to get you to where you want to go. Following the "Go All In" principle will ensure your success regardless of your life situation, talents, skills, education, or the current financial situation you are in. Use this book as though your life and dreams depended on it and you'll learn to accelerate to a higher level faster than you ever thought possible! *Go All In* will guide you toward a new frame of mind that understands that even if you come up short, you'll still find yourself much further along than where you are at right now.

Go All In teaches you how to:
- Set the right mindset and define precise goals before you even start.
- Create a level of success that helps you become a role model for yourself because **you're** the one who gets to create your dreams. You are the master and the conductor of your own dreams and your dream life.
- Get rid of fear and procrastination. You'll develop a new response habit, punch fear in the face, and move directly toward your goals.
- Reach the goals that even you and everyone around you previously thought were impossible.

Instead of dreaming about what could be — or wishing that someone or something would magically appear in your life that would make it easier — you need to create success for yourself. It is your duty and obligation, and by taking massive actions and going all in, you will create more success than you ever dreamed of!

"Keep crushing it!"

SECTION ONE
Decisions are Everything

Can you identify something you want passionately?
What are you aiming for: a personal breakthrough or
"more of the same things"?
Do you realize you are already prepared to do big things?

"I want to be successful in my career and finances, but I'm scared I'm gonna screw up."

Man, that voice replayed in my head for many years and kept me from going out and doing the things I wanted to do. That fear kept me from living my day-to-day life, unable to take one blow at a time with the liberty to figure out what I should be doing at that moment. I didn't know how to plan ahead. I was unhappy, unsatisfied, and sick. I was living like a chronically anxious person for many years. My days looked just like everyone else's. I got up in the morning, checked my phone and emails, and went to work for someone else's sake.

I was a yoga teacher, running around teaching yoga in five or six yoga studios and gyms throughout the day. Between my first class at 5 a.m. until my last class at 7 p.m., I was still bogged down with work. I left my home around 4:15 a.m. every morning to open the studio and then waited for students to shuffle in. I also worked at the front desk as an administrator on top of teaching. I would take breaks here and there throughout the day so that I could keep going until my last class which ended at 8. I'd then wait for every student to go home — although some of them wanted to have a lengthy chat after class — so by the time I got home, it was already close to 9 p.m. I continually missed out on time with my family; not to mention that the kids were usually already in bed by the time I got home. I hadn't even had dinner with my family for many years! What a life!

I never wanted to end up like that, but somehow I got by like this for many years. I thought I was living my dream, but it wasn't a dream come true — it was just a fantasy I thought I had wanted. My actions didn't align with my dream for myself and what I wanted for my life.

I was surviving like this until I said to myself, "I'm sick of being sick, tired, and broke!" What was my solution then? Get off the sofa, get out of the house, and get into a new way of thinking. I made my way into the market, sought out opportunities, got in front of potential clients, and showed them what I could do. I was applying the concept of "I need to be seen to sell".

My life started to change because I was sick of the way things were — of being broke financially and emotionally. I needed to restore so many things: my health, my relationships, my marriage; but it was that sickness that woke me up and let me know that I needed to shift into wellness.

The opportunities started to open right away. In fact, they were there for me to discover as soon as I started looking. I started to meet the right people, the right mentors, the right friends at the exact time that I was seriously seeking and needing them. I attended a lot of networking groups just to get myself out there and connect with other people who do what I do, and who have similar goals and passions as I have.

Once I made the decision to go all in and started getting traction, I had so much fun adding more wood to my fire that I promised myself I wouldn't stop until I "burned the place down". I didn't rest. I didn't stop until I succeeded. By taking action, I started a self-perpetuating momentum. Like a flywheel: once it gets going, it's going to continue. Once I started pedaling and building up speed, I couldn't stop that forward momentum.

I want you to know that you can experience the same fun I had working, but you need to give yourself a chance to go all in and go full-out. You need to give it your 100% focus, and you need to believe now, more than ever, that you can succeed. Believing that you can is the most important thing you can do for yourself.

Once you make the decision to commit to your goals and take effective actions, you will be able to see exponential improvement in your performance. You will multiply your personal effectiveness, hit new highs, and shatter your own achievement records. You don't have to settle for things as they are now. Things can change dramatically. If you are ready to make that decision, life is prepared to give you a breakthrough experience. You can jump to a higher level of achievement, live the dream, and enjoy a successful life. Make the decision that you are going to change your personal rules for success. You've got to shift gears and follow a new pattern of thought and action. Let's do this!

Featured on both TV and in magazines, Nim was also a guest for many podcast interviews.

1.
THERE IS NO SHORTAGE OF SUCCESS

There is no limit as to how much success you can create, but you need to have an "I can do it!" attitude.

The way you view success is just as important as how you approach success.

You can have as much as you want in this world and so can I. Unfortunately, most people look at success as something hard to achieve or something that luck allots only to certain people. The truth is, there is no limit to the number of ideas, creativity, talent, or opportunities available in the world. Intelligence, originality, persistence, and determination make the difference.

Success is something we create, not acquire. Unlike silver, copper, gold, or diamonds that are created naturally; success isn't something you go out and discover. It won't appear in your life until you work for it and build it up. In other words, success is something that you make happen and there is no shortage to the amount of success you can make. Everyone can have success and everyone can be successful, but you first need to believe that it's possible. Afterward, you take consistent inspired action to make it happen for you.

One of the reasons a lot of people have difficulties achieving their goals is that most have what I call "short-term thinking". We tend to dream too small. We only think about what we can achieve under the current circumstances. We are already limiting ourselves from the start. However, once you can erase the concept of short-term thinking or small step-by-step actions, you will find that by being a "Big Thinker", you'll overcome all your obstacles.

One experience I've had of thinking too small is one that I, unsurprisingly, regret. When I was twenty, a friend in my dance company told me about a really big dream of his. He told me he wanted to become the most successful dancer — the most well-known internationally. I told him that while that sounded nice, I just wanted to stay in Thailand. I was content to be able to dance on the local stage. Honestly, I was hoping to just continue with that dance job for a long time. I didn't have a bigger picture or a specific plan. There was no game plan or growth plan. I only hoped to continue doing what I had already been doing. On the other hand, my friend took massive action and got accepted to Cirque du Soleil — the world-famous Montreal-based entertainment company, and the largest contemporary circus producer in the world. He became one of the top 30 most successful circus performers in the world. Meanwhile, I was still where I was. Nothing had changed or improved for my dance career or for me, personally. That's why I tell my clients to always think of what they want in life. Have a big goal and a dream destination. I say, "Think as BIG as you can. Dream as big as you can, because it will drive your energy to get excited, get you out of bed to pursue your dreams each day."

Over the past few years, I have met with a great many entrepreneurs who are extremely knowledgeable in their field, have years of experience working with the leaders in their field, and have prepared themselves to be rockstars for a long time. However, these entrepreneurs constantly say, "I'm too busy", and are convinced that they never have the time to focus on building their business the way they clearly desire. Ahh, too many people make too many excuses! See, when you make excuses, you are allowing the failure effect to come. You may not have even started and could already be setting yourself up to fail by getting in the habit of making excuses.

The "Go All In" principle is the opposite of giving the same comfortable response of "Oh, I'm going to do it later." No! You need to focus and get it done right now. If you want to be successful in a business that you love, you need to commit to planning, working hard, taking action, and to keep going. If you want to improve your relationship with your partner, parent, or child; you'll probably need to spend a lot of quality time talking, understanding, and forgiving each other.

However, if you don't really take what you want to accomplish seriously, you don't have to take my advice. Going all in requires the mind to be strong. The heart must long for your desired destination and the body must follow up saying, "I will do whatever it takes".

Going all in is not a gift or a talent. It's not about education or money. It's a commitment — a decision. You say that you are going to do it, and you do it.

2.
BE UNCOMFORTABLE

Going all in is an act of faith. It's exhilarating and scary at the same time.

I want you to know that this decision will make you feel uncomfortable because it is a new journey.

However, when you own the end result with your conviction, confidence, and desire to see that end result actualized; nothing can shake your faith. Whatever you want to achieve, I would love to ask you to go all in. Go at it full-out because the results you are longing for are waiting for you!

One of my mentors, Jesse Johnson, would always say, "Everything you want is already yours." When you make the decision to go beyond other people's limiting beliefs as well as your own, you are going for the breakthrough. When the fear kicks in, you will start making a lot of excuses. You will listen to the fears and logical excuses coming up freely in response. You can easily convince yourself that the growth is not a good step for you because it is potentially a terrible mistake. But you have to move beyond the fear and take decisive action to become more confident. This is the only way you will learn the skills to master your own game and create real success for yourself.

While 80% of people live their lives with too many excuses because they are afraid to fall, 20% know that they might fail, but will find a way to ultimately succeed regardless of possible setbacks. These are the people who do things that are initially very uncomfortable to them. They stretch themselves anyway because they also know that they will ultimately be successful. Any failure they face will be overcome with persistence. Guess which category the most successful entrepreneurs and game changers are in?

Use intention to shape your future. You have to carry your faith as you travel beyond the comfort of your familiar, everyday reality — so press on. Now is the time for you to do something with the inertia created by the decisions you've made. Claim the end result now as you begin to create the path to reach it. The commitment you made will help your faith grow and light up the fire in your heart. "Go all in" is the passionate statement of how you care for the thing you are seeking. Remember, your passion and your emotions will hold the power to carry you to the path you seek. Let your decision to go all in take charge of your body in order to take the next action required to achieve your goals. Go for it instead of taking forever to get ready!

The feeling of "I'm not ready" is a result of anxiety. If you wait until you are ready, you will never do it at all. It's time to start now. Going all in can only happen in the present. Most people will say, "It is impossible.", but you will say, "It's possible." Whatever you want to do or be is your best possibility. However, only through making a decision to go all in will you take the necessary actions and finally transform your dreams into reality.

What happens next? The fear will kick in. Of course it will kick in the moment you start doing something new while holding a vision that is bigger than anything you've ever tried before. That's what happens with New Year's resolutions, for example. It's mostly a short-term commitment. You make the decision to change a habit and feel great, but then the fear kicks in and you stop yourself. You have to punch fear in the face.

I know you're scared. I'm scared too. Honestly, if you aren't scared, your goal is too small. Fear is a sign that you're doing something new. The goal means a lot to you, and it's a huge undertaking, so of course it will scare you. Of course the actions you will be required to take will make you feel uncomfortable. But if your goal is not big enough, it won't change much in you. It won't alter your emotions or your actions. You may not even need a plan and will wing it because you don't really need one. That's not the kind of goal that will challenge you and transform your life. I'm talking about realizing your big dreams and going after your passion. If your goal isn't big enough to make you scared, you're not challenging yourself enough.

However, you can use fear to your advantage. Fear can be a tool to dive into where you want to go if you don't run away from it. We're trained to move in the opposite direction whenever we feel fear pop up even just a little bit. Prepare yourself for this experience. You are going to discover some unfamiliar feelings you've never faced before. At times you may wonder if the situation is about to spin out of control. Sometimes you'll feel uncomfortable because those around you are starting to criticize what you do and you just want to quit. I want you to know that you are not alone and you are doing something that will lead you toward a bigger achievement — so press on.

One day, I was doing my own thing posting some of my success stories in one of my mentor's Facebook groups when I ended up inviting her clients to know more about my business. Well, my mentor suddenly contacted me and told me that I couldn't cross the boundaries by inviting her clients to join my group and work with me. I was a hundred percent scared because I felt like I did something bad unintentionally. I wasn't thinking very well and didn't see that it was a big deal; but from her perspective, it was crossing a boundary. I was so scared at first that I seriously thought of running away from the community, never contacting my mentor again, and just pretending that nothing happened. I didn't want to face the issue or her. However, I also knew that I needed to be professional if I wanted to play a bigger game for my business. I needed to play like a professional.

I sat with my feeling of fear instead of running away and decided to do the right thing and contact my mentor. I reached out to her and apologized because I didn't mean to cross those boundaries and promised her I would never do anything like that again — then something amazing happened. I moved from fear to creativity and got a great business idea. I invited her to be my partner in the coaching program I offered at the time and we would split the profit. She saw how much I committed to it, and she saw how I didn't give up and kept punching fear in the face so she said, "YES" and joined my big project. We both won the game! We found a perfect fit for both of us and we were both equally excited. It turned out to be a great success.

Another great example of moving beyond the fear to success comes from a client of mine, Ruby, who was ready to go all in with her business but found it extremely difficult to move beyond her fear of failure since she had tried and failed many times. She had invested a lot of money in her endeavors and was afraid of losing more money. Ruby wanted to succeed but she was full of doubt. She kept canceling our start date. She was afraid that she wouldn't be able to afford it, even though she was investing in exactly the help she needed to level-up her business and start earning those six figures — for which she was more than ready and capable of. She wanted it and believed she was destined to achieve it, and yet she would stop herself before she started that one last time because the fear of failure — due to her past experiences —

was greater than the belief that she could succeed this time.

No one else can do it for you. No one else can overcome that fear for you. That fearful voice in your head that keeps repeating: "What if I lose all this money?" "What if he says no?" "What if I never lose this weight?" This fearful voice affects your body. Your breathing becomes short and shallow, and you tense up. If you aren't careful, you can let the fear run away with you. Soon you'll be convinced that this isn't a passing emotion but your eternal truth. However, you must always remind yourself that this is not a permanent state — it's temporary. It doesn't have a say in your long-term plans.

So instead of feeling sad or sorry for yourself when fear pops up, I invite you to step out of your comfort zone and out of your fear zone. Fear is not a bad thing. Fear comes up because you need to step up. It's telling you to step up.

Use fear as fuel to move forward. You wanted to make a change, so make the decision — not just to try or to see how it goes.

Fear is a part of daily reality. Your confidence grows as a result. Fear pushes you to do better and take action, so fear is your friend. Fear a sign that you're stepping up and moving into new territory to build your success.

I feel purposeful every day because my focus is full of intent. I don't put up with dramas and time-wasters because I know that they shift my attention from where I want to go. I choose to stay energized and focused.

I used to be "all over the place". I thought of many amazing ideas that excited me, dreamed up scenarios that would be amazing to experience, but didn't take a lot of action to build my road to that destination. I put a lot of energy into the "thinking" mode but not in the "doing" mode, so unsurprisingly, I just ended up overthinking and never seeing results.

I would tell almost anyone who would listen about my dreams: my family, my friends, and even people I didn't even know very well. I really was "all over the place" — sharing my vision with people who couldn't understand or share my dream. They'd say it was too risky, too big, too soon, too expensive; and I ended up believing them. I would tell myself that it wasn't possible because nothing was happening.

Success requires a process. The process starts when we show up and act on the ideas we get. Fear is part of the process. It always shows up. But when I began to "punch fear in the face", I started to shift that habit and become very focused. This was the shift I needed.

Many years ago, I wanted to start my own business but had no idea what I really wanted to do. I hadn't determined my niche, or who exactly I served, so I never figured out what it would take to grow. That was until I found my mentor and she taught me how to build a coaching business. Because I made the decision to go all in for this coaching business and implement everything she taught me, I learned many new skills and systems. I even surprised myself by getting real results within just a few months. Being focused is now my second nature.

Stay Focused! Going all in is a duty — a responsibility and an obligation. If this was a life or death situation, then you know you will do all it takes in order to make things work. This is what it means to "Go All In". First, you make the decision to go all in and then you find a way to make it happen — and that's when things really start to happen.

Exercise:

1. What are your biggest fears in life?
2. What holds you back when you are moving toward a new goal that you haven't achieved yet, but you have desired for a long time?
3. What makes you pause once you start working toward what you want? Reflect on what deep fear keeps you from pushing too far.
4. Where do you feel it in your body?
5. Who do you know that could help you overcome that fear and push you forward to your results?
6. What did you learn about fear in this chapter?

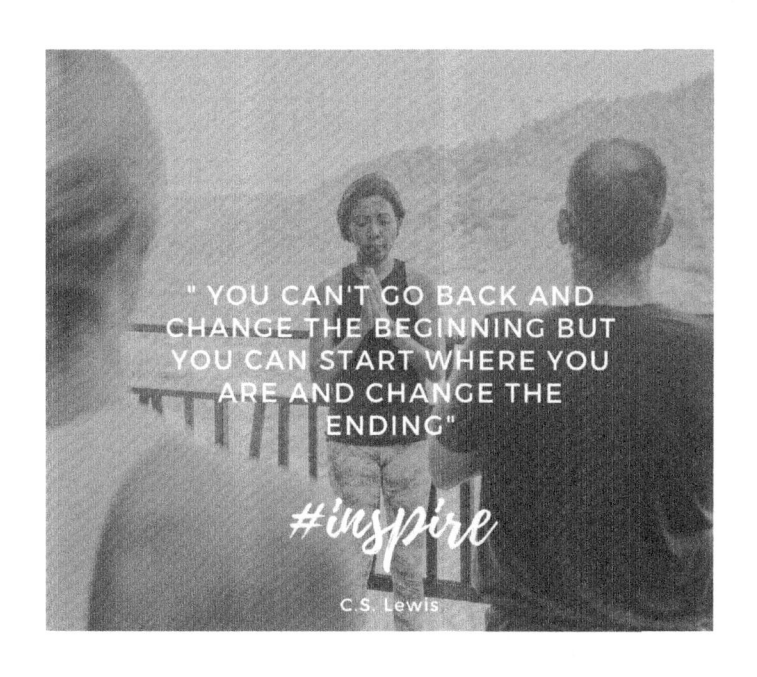

> "YOU CAN'T GO BACK AND CHANGE THE BEGINNING BUT YOU CAN START WHERE YOU ARE AND CHANGE THE ENDING"
>
> #inspire
>
> C.S. Lewis

3.
COMMIT FIRST, FIGURE OUT LATER

You don't need to know how you'll get there; you need to know where you want to go.

When I started my business, I hoped that I would make 10k a month — that I would be that successful. I hoped that I would make enough money to pay off the debt I had, or at least pay off the latest investments I had made in my business. "I hope…" is not an action.

Act and things shift. Make changes and commit. Get up earlier in the morning and stay up later at night in order to put in the extra work that needs to be done. I have no problem spending extra time focusing on my goal because that way, I know that I will get it done. If it takes five years, then so be it; but I'm not giving up until I see what I want manifesting. This mindset shift was a game-changer for me. I no longer hoped that it would work out because I owned the end destination I desired which was working my successful six-figure business from home. That was then, and now I have a new goal that is a level-up from that.

I want to own a farmhouse with a big space in the backyard. I will work from my computer for a few hours every morning and then go into the garden and enjoy my animals. I will ride my horses. I want to travel the world with my kids to show them the world without ever worrying about the cost of airfare and hotels. I want my company to be available for my kids — if they choose to help manage it — so they learn how to be entrepreneurs while they're still young.

Once I committed to the vision I held around my goal, I immediately felt a difference in my body. Something shifted. My commitment and certainty became a sensation I couldn't ignore. I felt both excited and grounded — more solid and firm in my presence, even though I was nervous. I knew that I would get there and it didn't matter how long it took. Knowing that I would get there made me lock in on this destination. It felt really good to be this certain. I added more details to my vision of the end result since I felt confident that somehow I would get there. I dreamed a little bigger, relaxed, and worked steadily toward that goal. I got there not in five or ten years but in nine months.

You don't need to know how you're going to get there, but you need to know where you want to go. If you want to lose fifty pounds, you've got to know the fifty pound part — the number and the goal. You don't need to know how much water you need to drink nor how many calories you need to burn and eat each day yet. If you just say I want to lose weight, that's not a target. That's not a specific goal. You need to know where the arrow is going to hit before you let it fly. You don't need to know exactly how the air is moving and the arrow's resistance or anything like that. You need to simply keep your eye on the target.

The world behaves differently when you actually take action to go after what you want. Your dreams begin to manifest. What you are seeking starts to move in your direction. It begins to come to you as you reach for it. This is not about living a little more comfortably, paying off debts, and getting a better car. This is much more than that. This is your legacy.

So when you make the decision that you will do whatever it takes to get to your goals, your inner energy will clear up the path for you. You might notice that out of nowhere the exact people you need to meet just show up in your life. Remember, knowing where you want to go is the first most important step. You are trusting the power of an unseen force.

A few years ago in 2003, I met professor Sadchidaanan Sahai at a seminar I attended. He gave a talk on Indian architecture. At that time, I was very interested in going to India to start dancing over there, but I had no idea how I could make such a trip happen. I went to the seminar because India fascinated me and I wanted to learn more about it. I listened to his talk intently, paid full attention to what he said; and at the end of the seminar, something amazing happened. He walked directly to me and asked, "Do you want to study in India?" Oh boy! I was so startled and excited that I just kept saying, "Yes, sir… Yes, sir!" He then helped me network and introduced me to the exact people I needed to be in contact with. Finally, he wrote a recommendation for me, which helped me get selected for a scholarship from the Indian Embassy.

See, when you put your focus and energy on what you want to accomplish, the path will open and the right people will appear at exactly the right moment. However, if you put your focus or your energy on the wrong thing or hang out with the wrong group of people, you're going to get results that reflect the quality of whatever you put your focus on.

If you are on the right path, you will start to see results from your action. Your customers might start to show up, wanting to work with you, and you'll begin to have your starting breakthrough for your business. The path will open and it will be something you didn't plan for beforehand. Once you make the decision to go all in, your journey begins, and shifts happen.

Going all in is an act of faith because you accept the end result as a certain fact, even before you can see it. It feels good to be charged up and committed, but it feels uncomfortable too. Making the decision to go all in is scary. To go all in, you will have to give up a large part of your old patterns. You will need to give up a large degree of security and safety. It won't sound so great when you first hear this, but to go all in, you are actually inviting failure into your life. You will very possibly receive criticism from people close to you and who play a big part in your life. That's why it's so important to realize that "Fear and criticism are a sign of success."

Don't run away and give up yet. Commit to it now and start to see positive changes. Someday as you look back and connect the dots, you will see that going all in means knowing that some days you will fail, but the fall won't stop you. You keep on going, daring to do it anyway. You are committing to your goals 100%.

For many years, I knew that I wanted to share my message on TV, but didn't know how to do it. I looked for a mentor who could teach me. After a few weeks of learning, I decided to make a big move by writing an email pitch to the TV producer for the Motivational Monday Show on TV3 in Arizona. At the same time, I took another scary step by calling the news-desk and asking for the producer's contact. After I reached out to the producer directly — which was completely out of my comfort zone — the producer responded by asking if I was available for an interview the following Monday. So, not only was that a "BIG YES" from the producer, but she also invited me to be on two shows on the same day. For me, that "BIG YES" was a reminder that if I committed first, everything else would open up for me. I didn't need to know how to start. I could figure it out later.

Exercise:

1. Write in your journal. Why is being successful and living your best life important to you?
2. Imagine specific changes you would like to see in your life.
3. How would they improve the quality of your life?
4. Write down a badass moment in your life. It can be something that you are proud of doing for your business, for your health, or for any aspect of your personal life.

Just as an example, here is my list of 10 badass moments:

1. I was able to order a strawberry milkshake from McDonald's and they gave me exactly what I asked for. It meant a lot to me that people in America understood my English.
2. When I studied dance in India, I was the only foreigner in the University, yet I received the highest grade in the whole dance department. It took me less than a year to learn the dances and be skillful enough that I could compete with native students.

3. I hosted yoga retreats in Thailand that brought people from all over the United States to my home country.

4. I wrote and published my first book in English.

5. People I've never met Google my name and buy my book.

6. I helped my kids learn to play the piano, and they're very good now.

7. I've coached many people to build their business around their passion and guided them to accomplishment.

8. Kajabi interviewed me and wrote an article focusing on how I pivoted my business during the COVID-19 pandemic.

9. I went outdoor rock climbing. It was scary, but a very fun moment.

10. Any time my kids say to me, "You're the best mom.", and kiss me.

Go beyond the handbook! Focus on The Ends rather than The Means. The key is not to get in the way.

—Price Pritchett,
You2: A High-velocity Formula for Multiplying Your Personal Effectiveness in Quantum Leaps

SECTION TWO
Get Super Clear

It is very important to have a crystal clear picture of what you want to have or accomplish. Visualize your arrival. For now, all you need is an aiming point. You'll follow it up with action later. For the moment, you need to focus.

Start by coming up with a clear picture of your goal in your mind. Create a mental picture and don't just think about it. Be sure to add all the feelings you have when you imagine reaching this goal. What emotions will you feel when you achieve everything you want right now? Keep it alive in your mind. The reason I ask you to create a crystal clear aiming point is that I want you to be laser-focused on that end goal. I want you to work toward achieving it, rather than thinking about *how you are going to achieve it.*

It's easy to get lost when you have ten different goals, are feeling overwhelmed and confused, and are caught juggling too much. That won't get you anywhere. *Be exact, be specific, be clear.* And remember, don't get in your way! When you set a goal like exercising to lose weight but then you get tripped up by a tiny problem that comes up — like not having a water bottle or the right headphones for the gym — you use this as an excuse not to take action. This is how you get in your own way. Don't do that!

I encourage you to think bigger and bigger about your goal until it makes you feel uneasy. Why? Because in the next 30 or 365 days, you will need to work hard to achieve your goal despite being uncomfortable. If you set your goals or your standards too low, it won't motivate you enough. Along the way, there will be cynics, downers, and critics. However, no one can convince you that you can't do it if you don't say it to yourself first. The negative thoughts in your head will hurt you more than those expressed by other people. Protect yourself because you're vulnerable while building your dream. You have to hold onto your dreams so fiercely that nothing will shake you from your goal. People around you will say, "It's too risky!" Of course they will! It is because they've never done anything like this. If those around you doubt your abilities, don't let it stop you. Just keep moving and soon you will be so far beyond the naysayers that you won't be able to hear them anymore.

So forget what other people think for a moment and ask yourself:

What do I really want?
What is it that my heart needs?
What will feed my soul?

If becoming a better mom is what you really want to work on, and your heart says, "*Yes, I want to go all in to become a better mom.*", then picture it in your mind. What picture do you see as you visualize it? Draw that imaginary picture of your goal and keep it alive by visualizing it every day and throughout each day. Say what you want to achieve — your specific goal — to yourself throughout the day.

"There is no one right path. There are endless paths, and the differences in the paths are what make them more and more, and more perfect."

—Abraham Hicks

4.
POWER OF GOALS

When your beliefs are aligned with your desire, a new direction will show up, solutions will appear and answers will come to you.

Beliefs → Thoughts → Feelings → Actions = Outcomes

Everything we perceive, interpret, create, and experience as our reality is filtered through what we believe is or is not possible. We know the value of setting goals: long-term goals, short-term goals, daily goals, monthly goals, personal goals, organizational goals, ten-year goals, lifetime goals, etc. Goal-setting is a powerful process and it helps us focus our energy and concentrate on the end result we seek. However, if you want to make goal setting really work for you, you need to know the *what* and the *why*.

Let's look at these individually.

What?

What do I desire to accomplish? What is the contribution I want to make? What is the end I have in mind? The difference is what you chose to focus on. What you seek, you generally find. When you set goals that are in harmony with your conscience and principles, you naturally create the quality of life you seek and find the best way to get there.

Why?

Ask yourself: why do I want it? Does my goal empower me to contribute to my roles? Creating self-awareness and empowerment involves deep personal honesty. It comes from asking yourself and answering these honest questions:

Do I really want it?
Do I really want to do it?
Am I willing to pay the price?

Do I accept responsibility for my own growth?

Self-awareness prompts us to start from where we are — no excuses — and help us set empowerment goals. I talk to myself every morning when I first wake up. I repeat, "I am willing. I am open. I am able. I can." These are the empowerment words that I use for setting up my mind to be ready to go about my day. Focusing on what is possible is very important.

A lot of people focus on what they can't do rather than what they can. You need to use the power of your mind to help you work on how to achieve your goals. However, if you don't have any goal or don't know what you really want, chances are you won't achieve it. If you don't have a clear goal, you may not even realize you've already achieved it.

Next, write it down on paper or find the picture that will represent or symbolize this goal. Put it where you know you will see it often throughout the day, every day. I know, you've probably heard of or read about this in a lot of books already — but the point is that it works. If you don't do it, no one will get mad at you, but you just won't see the results you want.

Finally, as a daily ritual, spend time looking at the word you wrote or the picture you used to symbolize your goal so that your mind remembers the outcome you seek.

To set and work toward any goal is an act of courage. When we exercise the courage to set and act on goals, we tend to achieve positive results. This is the process of growth — of becoming all we are born to be.

Focus on the specific outcome you seek. Be super clear in your mind what you really want and need. Then treat intention as an active and positive force that takes you to where you want to be. The key is to let the future know what you really want to happen, specifically.

"The future rewards those who press on. I don't have time to feel sorry for myself. I don't have time to complain. I'm going to press on."

—Barack Obama

You can use the power of your subconscious mind to help you get what you want. I use it every day — especially in the morning. It's like I'm talking to my future self. I form the sentence based on what I want to accomplish and then say it to myself. The words I tell myself are things I imagine have already happened or obtained.

It's been several years now since I started telling myself every day that "I am well and healthy." Before I started doing that, I was sick every month. There was always some new problem that showed up. First, I had broken my toe. Next, a toy thrown during my kids' playdate left me with a black eye that lasted for weeks. After that, I had ended up with walking pneumonia that left me alone in my bedroom for over two weeks because no one could be close to me. I asked myself, "*How did I get here?*" and then I realized that I had been saying to myself, "*I'm sick and unwell.*" instead of "*I am well and healthy.*" every day. No wonder that's exactly how my body responded. So I've made it a habit to say, "*I am well and healthy.*" every day when I wake up and throughout the day.

Notice that I don't say, "*I'm not sick.*" because sick is a negative word. Debt-free is not the best choice of words either. It's better to say, "*I have financial freedom.*" I chose to change what I said to myself first thing in the morning when I had just opened my eyes and was still lying down and waking up. That choice changed everything.

I no longer have accidents or illnesses because my body is already listening to me. It has become something that I don't even think about anymore because I am doing well every day. Of course I get tired from time to time. But if I lie down to rest for a short while, my body will feel balanced and restored right away. I haven't gone to the doctor for several years now. I just don't get sick any more. I still do this every day — I do this in the morning and keep saying it throughout the day, whenever I can remember.

This works because your brain receives your thoughts. The brain is the organ of your conscious reasoning mind. When your conscious mind accepts the thought completely, a signal is sent to the solar plexus — also called the abdominal brain — where it becomes flesh and is made manifest in your experience. Your subconscious mind only acts from what you write on it so if your body is well, your subconscious mind can not argue otherwise. As the American essayist, Ralph Waldo Emerson said, "A man is what he thinks about all day long."

Retreats hosted in Thailand.

5.
YOU HAVE TO GIVE UP TO GROW UP

"If we don't change, we don't grow. If we don't grow, we aren't really living." —Gail Sheehy

Setting a goal is a very exciting thing to do and it's NOT hard for many people to set a goal. They make an agreement with themselves to commit to their goal but don't end up achieving it because they weren't aware of the inconveniences that they have to go through as they work toward their goal. The inconvenience is the thing that makes many people angry and disappointed, leaving them to give up on their dreams and goals. The questions we all should ask ourselves as we set our goals are, what will it take for me to go to the next level? Vision? Hard work? What do I need to let go of? Do I need to let go of some of the things that I love and value the most? Am I willing to give up those things for a chance at doing something that will take me closer to my potential?

I often hear people expressing the hope that things will change. In those moments, I want to tell them that the difference between where we are and where we want to be is created by the changes we are willing to make in our lives. When you want something you never had, you must do something you've never done to get it. Otherwise, you will keep getting the same results. Changes to our lives always begin with changes we are willing to make personally.

Achieving goals requires making changes. When we no longer can change our situation, we are challenged to change ourselves. One of the toughest personal changes I went through was last year in 2019. I found myself at an intersection in my life. I realized that one of the ways for me to reach more people and sharing my message is to write a book. Well, English isn't my native language, and writing isn't my best skill either. However, I decided to write a book anyway. I started reading many books and researching different information that will support my book. It took me days and nights to write, to rewrite, hundreds of pages of manuscript. For the first three months, I spent so many hours a day working on my book, finishing it, and publishing it. In the end, it did pay off. I was able to publish my first book. Did I make a lot of money from writing that book? No. But it put me on the road to reaching my full potential because I grew and I improved. Today, I'm writing my second book and I know that there will be a third, fourth, fifth, and many more books written by me.

This transition can be a real challenge. Most of us want to see the outcome right away. The change or the trade-off feels like a loss. Some people deal with uncertainty very well, but some don't. You must choose to have a positive attitude and focus on the upcoming benefits of the trade-off.

Here are a few good questions to ask yourself when it comes to growth and success:
Am I willing to give up the fast life for a good life?
Am I willing to give up security for significance?
Am I willing to give up addition for multiplication?

Write your own personal answers in your journal and remember to revisit your journal and read your answer every day or as often as you can.

"I believe that unsuccessful people make bad trade-offs, average people make few trade-offs, and successful people make good trade-offs."
—John C. Maxwell

6.
EMPOWERMENT FROM THE INSIDE OUT

"It's not about how much you do, but how much love you put into what you do that counts."
—Mother Teresa

Do you love what you do?

In this chapter, I want to talk specifically about new entrepreneurs out there. I have been coaching so many passionate women who really want to become successful in what they do, but the problem is they let fear stay in their way. So many of them tell me that they will need to work on their nine-to-five jobs first, and then they will follow their passion and work for building their dream business on the side. So I asked, why are you doing that? Why do you believe that you need to do nine-to-five jobs first, and then work on the things that you love after? Most of them answered that it is because they are afraid that they won't make it. They don't believe they can make their dream business work, therefore they are willing to stay in a job that drains their energy every day to support their dream jobs.

This doesn't make any sense to me. I don't believe that this system and plan will work!

Let's get real here, we're all going to die. You, me, and every single person we know. Whether it's in days, months, or hopefully many years from now, we're all on a train heading to the same destination. Every single moment is very important, so don't waste your time working on something you don't have any love for. We're always one step closer to taking our final breath. I'm not saying this to depress you, I'm saying this to inspire you. **Our time on the earth is extremely limited and precious. YOU are extremely precious. Believe in yourself and**

get out to do what you love. Do not waste your life working on something you don't love and care about just for the money or just to please others.

God and the universe put you here on the earth for a reason. God gave you the unique blend of talents, strengths, and perspectives that you have. Deep down, you know there's something special you're meant to do in this world. Whatever your dream is, whatever is the call of your soul, whatever that thing is that makes you, you — let that love in your heart move you. Let it fire you up. Let it inspire you. Let that love be your driving motivation.

When you are working on what you love, others around you can be motivated by your drive. They will see a deep love for your goal and will see that you are meant for some kind of meaningful contribution that will make a difference in the world. I adore what I do and wake up every morning extremely grateful for my business, our customers — that includes you — our team, and my family.

The practice of "Going All In" will not work if you only use your brain to logically think and plan your success. It takes your heart too — your whole heart — to commit fully. Remember, we are aiming for 100% results and we are talking about 100% full-out action. Therefore, you need 100% of your heart to be there too!

Why use the "Go All In" principle doing something that you hate? That doesn't make any sense. When you are in love with someone and want to know that person better because you want to be with them and share your life with them, you are going all in with all your heart. This is the same thing you need to do with whatever you want to accomplish. Put your whole heart in it!

I actually found that it is more fun to work hard on something that I love and am passionate about. I don't feel tired as easily. In fact, I have all the energy in the world and no regrets — just like writing this book right now. It is so much fun because I love doing it from the bottom of my heart. I enjoy the process. I want to leave a legacy, so I decided to get out of my own way and go for it.

I observed that there are three kinds of people when it comes to having direction in life:
1. People who don't know what their heart wants to do.
2. People who know what their heart wants to do, but don't do it.
3. People who know what their heart wants to do, and they do it.

Knowing what your heart wants isn't necessarily an easy thing for every person to do. The best way to start is to pay close attention to your passions then ask yourself these questions:

1. Do I like what I'm doing right now?
2. What would I like to do?
3. Can I do what I would like to do?
4. Do I know the difference between what I want and what I'm good at?
5. Do I know what drives me and what gives me satisfaction?

Exercise:

Let's focus on your biggest goal or dream because that is the one that you need to plan out right now. So, which one is it? What is your heart calling out for?

1. Spend some quiet time alone. Define a specific goal you want to achieve.

Remember, you can have it all.

You can have everything you want: good health, romantic relationships, a successful career, financial freedom — you name it. You can have it all, but you need to know what your "it" is — what you want — and what your "all" is — everything you want to become and experience.

If you say, "I just want to be happy." What does your version of "happy" look like? For some people, that is having $1,000,000 in their bank account. For others, it's their son being accepted into a good school on a scholarship. Another person's happiness is losing fifty pounds and buying a new wardrobe. It's great if you're saying, "I want to have it all!", but be sure to define very specifically what that looks like for you.

Create a mental picture and write it down as if you have already achieved it. Imagine exactly what you want to achieve in as clear and concise a description as you can. Don't worry if you can't think of how you will achieve your goal. It isn't time to worry about it yet. Focus on what you really want to happen.

Write down how you will feel when you get it. Write in every detail of how it will make you feel.

For example:

"I am so happy and thankful that money comes to me easily and effortlessly.
 People hire me and pay me really really well!
 I have all the money I need and I share it with my charity to support others.
 I have an abundance of time and money.
 I am so happy that I am now an eight-figure business owner.
 I love what I do and how I am able to help tens of thousands of people from all over the world."

Put some images on the paper and keep your positive energy moving as you imagine your goal.

2. Collect images such as some photos or magazine cut-outs that symbolize your goals or create a digital collage, print it out, and hang it on your wall. This is a vision board and it reminds you of what you want to see in your life. When you are working on this and writing your goals down, stay in a place where you can stay focused and bring the experience alive in your mind.

3. Read your goal out loud to yourself every morning, throughout your day, and before you go to bed. This way, you are creating a ritual to remind yourself which direction you are actually aiming for. You'll remember where you are going, and how you are moving toward your goals.

4. Write the date you started your ritual. This way, you can keep track of your unique process and how it unfolds as you open yourself to a new experience. Keep writing in your journal each day to remind yourself to focus on your end goals.

Slowly, you will discover the law of attraction by using your subconscious mind the right way. Writing the date you want to see things show up in your life is the way to manifest action and reaction. By specifying the time frame, you are telling the universe your intention. Your brain will order your body to take action. Your thought is the action, and the reaction will be the response of your subconscious mind where you "think", therefore you "become".

Your imagination is more powerful than your will.

SECTION THREE
Finding A Mentor

If you are in a room full of people and discover you're the smartest one, you are in the wrong room!

If you really want to be good at something, you need a mentor. A mentor will help you get to your goals and get results faster and even more effectively.

When I first made the decision to become very good at Ashtanga Yoga, I looked for a teacher who could not only show me how to do each posture correctly but also teach me the reasons why each posture was done in such a way, as well as the benefits for every posture. After all, a mentor isn't there to only show you how to do it. Your mentor also helps you stay in your lane. She gets you back on track when you get distracted and aren't moving forward.

There was a point in my life when I knew for sure that if I kept doing what I was doing as a yoga teacher, my business would fail. I didn't know when exactly, but I knew that someday it would because I was already so burned out from running around teaching at half a dozen studios. I wasn't sure which direction I should go from there, or how to continue making money as a yoga teacher. So I started to look everywhere — both online and in-person — for someone to teach me to become really good at running my yoga business.

I found my first business mentor from watching her YouTube channel. I checked her website and found that she was offering a group in-person intensive workshop for yoga teachers in Santa Monica. I booked a slot without hesitation to attend the workshop. That was the first start of business training for me. The coaching wasn't cheap, but I was willing to take the risk. I didn't have any money to pay, but I knew I would find the way and landed a financing option that worked.

I got so much more out of it than I even expected. I stayed in a small hostel and ate noodle cups for every meal during the training because I didn't have any extra money to spend. I had spent it all on the coaching and my flights to Santa Monica and back.

See, when I started my own business, I didn't have any money. I didn't have any connections nor business education. I didn't really have anything, BUT I knew that the one thing I had to have was a trusted guide who could show me the way to gain success. Otherwise, I would just keep losing money, trying too hard to figure it out on my own. If I hadn't hired a mentor, I know that I probably never would have become successful. At the very least, I would have taken *a lot longer* to get there.

76% of people think mentors are important, but only 37% have one. Why is that? Well, because they don't really go all the way in. It is easier to dream about the goals or talk about it, but it is a lot harder to really do it. Finding a mentor is another action step that you need to take if you really want to achieve your goal.

We don't know, what we don't know! Mentors provide a wealth of knowledge and experience. They guide us through challenges and increase our likelihood of success. They lift us up and take our success personally.

If you are wondering if you really need a mentor, ask yourself these two simple questions:

Are you about to do something new or make some changes in your life, but aren't really sure of how to do it?

Would you like to have a trusted and more experienced person to bounce ideas off, discuss challenges with, help you find the best ways to achieve specific goals, and help you save time and money?

If the answer is YES, then you would need to find someone who is an expert in the area you want to work on to become your mentor. However, it is very rare that find that person within your circle of friends or family.

I have an uncle in Thailand who I considered a mentor. I told my husband that my uncle is like my "rich dad" — like in the *Rich Dad Poor Dad* book. My uncle is a very successful businessman. He is very sharp. He plans well, thinks well, and really understands the art of negotiation. I watched his example for many years and followed in his footsteps. I asked him a lot of questions whenever I could and I always got answers that I could never come up with by myself. I also knew that I could trust him and that he would never look down at me.

If you can find someone to mentor you like this, that would be great! It takes a lot of trust and courage to tell someone about your dreams and goals. I have to protect my thoughts and my energy a lot when I'm around certain people. I don't really talk about my dreams and my goals with them because I know that they will never get it. They will tell me why it won't work and give opinions about things they know nothing about and have never done in their lives. That's why you need a mentor who will listen to you, guide you, and hold you accountable.

Research and surveys have proven that having a mentor is important to success. In a 2013 executive coaching survey, 80% of the CEOs said they received some form of mentorship. In another research by Sage, 93% of startups admit that mentorship is instrumental to success.

That should show you that the most successful people have help from experts in their field to reach their goals.

Why would you think that you need to do it all on your own? Your chances of success in life and in business will be amplified by having the right mentor. The valuable connections, timely advice, and regular check-ins — together with the spiritual and moral guidance you will gain from having a mentor — will literally leapfrog you to success.

My yoga mentor, "Kino MacGregor" — a world-class ashtanga yoga master.

7.
ASKING FOR HELP

The best decision I made for my business is to hire a mentor. If I wasted time trying to learn everything on my own, I would have just ended up "Learning But Never Earning".

You need a mentor! Of course hiring someone to teach you and help you reach your goals is going to cost money. Perhaps even a lot of money because there is nothing free in this world. However, the important thing is to think of it as an investment. It is a lifelong investment!

You should have a positive mindset. Don't say, "I can't afford a mentor". Instead ask yourself, "How can I afford to pay a mentor?" That subtle change of words is a huge shift in mindset. You have begun to find your way, and your journey has begun. You will realize later in your life that this was the point where everything changed because it was the moment you made that commitment to go all in and be held accountable.

Finding a mentor doesn't always have to cost money but you will need to ask for help. You may not know what to do — and would clearly benefit from some help — yet you won't or are afraid to ask for help. Most people either very reluctantly do so eventually, or decide to suffer in silence altogether.

Nod your head if you've ever had to ask for help at work, at home, or anywhere else. Now, nod again if you've ever felt shy or silly when doing so. Many of us automatically assume that asking for help, reading self-help books, or seeing a life coach means that something wrong or bad has happened or is happening in your life. The word help is regarded as negative BUT help is not a form of weakness or failure. Finding someone to help and teach you even when you are 40 years old is not a bad thing. I admire those who still keep learning throughout their life so much. Even the most successful people like Richard Branson and Warren Buffet ask for help and have other people advise them.

For the moment, take a look at an athlete as an example. Behind every successful athlete — or any athlete for that matter — is a coach. They are there to guide and train athletes on their path to achieving greatness. Coaches have the ability to point out blind spots and play on the athletes' strengths. While the athlete focuses on their current or specific training routine, the coach is already mapping out a bigger plan. That one training routine that the athlete is focusing on is but one of many more training routines that will eventually lead to the athlete succeeding and outperforming. Without the coach's vision to map that out and guide the athlete, the athlete will be training blindly, and not maximizing their efforts.

Do you see why we need to seek help in almost every area of our lives? If you are at a point in your life where you feel stuck and frustrated, that means it is time to find a mentor and ask for help. Don't wait until you are ready, have more time or money. Find the right mentor to help now and you won't regret it because you will already be on your way to your success. By taking an active step in seeking help or advice, you're actually taking control of your life and not letting external circumstances — such as what people think — affect how you behave and perform. It is courageous to accept your weaknesses!

"Whatever I have tried to do in life, I have tried with all my heart to do it well; whatever I have devoted myself to, I have devoted myself completely; in great aims and in small I have always thoroughly been in earnest."

—Charles Dickens

8.
If You Want to Be a Millionaire, Talk With a Billionaire

"More of the same" usually just gives you more of the same.

There is a quote from Peter Voodge — an extremely successful entrepreneur — that I love. He said, "If you want to be a millionaire you need to talk with a billionaire." He knew what he was talking about because he became a millionaire when he was just 26 years old, but the really interesting thing is that he had been learning from his mentor who became a millionaire when he was just 21 years old.

You see, whatever direction you want to go, whatever the one thing is that you want to achieve, I am pretty sure that you're not the only one who wants to achieve that specific goal in the world. I bet that there are many people who have achieved that same goal before you and are already successful living the result that you want to implement in your life. So what should you do then? Find them! You need to find that person who has been there and done it successfully. Get to know them, get close to them, and hire them to mentor you. It shouldn't be that hard or overly complicated. The online world is very powerful. Nowadays, you can Google and search for the exact people who already have the result you want, or perhaps that person is in your life already. You never know. Look around and you will find your mentor.

One woman heard about me from her friend and instantly googled my name. When she saw that I wrote the book *The Yoga Journey*, she bought it, read it, underlined it, and even took notes and studied it. She then signed up to come to my retreat in Thailand for 10 days because she wanted to meet me. During the retreat, she showed me her copy and asked me to sign it. I was impressed that she really studied my book. I was so thankful that I could impact someone like that. We had a very good, long conversation together and I shared with her that I can teach her how to overcome obstacles, follow her passion, and create the career of her dreams. So she signed up for my coaching program and I became her mentor. See, everything that happens to you and your life isn't an accident. You send your thoughts out and whatever you seek comes back to you!

When it comes to finding a mentor, you should seek someone who has done what you want to achieve before. A good mentor will challenge you as well as inspire you. That's their job! You're probably not going to grow until you get uncomfortable. Be ready to meet your mentor at any time. Remember, you don't necessarily need to have only one mentor. I have several mentors in different areas because I want to improve as many areas of my life as I can at the same time.

I have a mindset mentor, business mentor, social media mentor, and a health coach.

If you want to become successful at a new skill, no matter how large or small, you need to talk to those who have already succeeded and already had what you want. Your success doesn't start with what you do but starts with your mindset. So if you want to become a millionaire, it doesn't hurt to start thinking like them and talking to them. Well, you don't really have to find a millionaire or a billionaire unless it is your goal to become one. The point is, if you really want to be good and achieve something big, it makes total sense to talk to those who are already there at your goal.

A coach or mentor will teach you how to find your long-term goal — your life-long goal — because they can see the bigger picture. Long-term goals force you to grapple with big questions such as, "How can I double my income this year?" instead of short-term issues, such as, "How am I going to pay my bills this month?" Your coach or mentor will make sure that your focus is on the big things instead of the little things. You will also find that successful people are more willing to put temporary comfort on hold to seek out long-term success or freedom.

My very first investment was for me to learn from someone who already achieved the success I wanted for my business. It was a lot of money and it was scary to spend that much money but I never regretted it.

My mentor, now a 40-year-old woman, makes half of a million dollars per month. She is the founder of a multi-million dollar women's empowerment company. My business goal is to reach that height. My mentor is the same age as me but she's already where I want to be. Every time I get a chance to talk to her, learn from her, and see what she has done for her business; my world expands. I see what is possible for me and I believe that I can do it too.

If I had never sought out a mentor to show me how to position myself physically, emotionally, mentally, and financially; I would have never arrived at where I'm at today — with me writing this book and sharing my success with you.

Remember, if you are really serious and want to achieve something, you need to find someone to show you how. Mentors are people who allow you to see the hope inside yourself. A good mentor will help you become more of who you really are because they see more talent and ability within you than you see in yourself; and they will help bring it out of you.

Here are my favorite sayings, from achievers and millionaires, that have helped me stay focused on my goals and take the "go all in" action.

1. Never give up. Life can go from 0 to 100 real quick.
2. Do something different. Stand out from the crowd.
3. Don't stop when you are having a hard time, that's part of the deal.
4. Risk is the down payment on success.
5. You were born to make mistakes, not to fake perfections.
6. Luck is when preparation meets opportunity.
7. Success always comes down to one thing: How badly do you want it?
8. Work until your signature becomes your autograph.
9. The best way to predict the future is to create it.

10. Just because it takes you longer than others, doesn't mean you failed. Remember that.

Exercise:

Write down 3-5 people who you admire, and would love to have mentor you. Make a list of questions you would want to ask in order to learn from them.

Some questions to ask yourself:

1. Who do you want to learn from?
2. Who would you hire to mentor you?
3. Why do you want that person to mentor you?
4. How can they help you get to your goals?
5. Why is it so important for you to have a mentor?

"Change will not come if we wait for some other person or if we wait for some other time. We are the ones we've been waiting for. We are the change that we seek."

—Barack Obama

Behind the scenes at Go All In TV: Interviewing Deb Richardson, a U.S. Olympian.

9.
What to Look for in a Mentor

"Your mentors in life are important, so choose them wisely."

—Robert Kiyosaki, Rich Dad Poor Dad

It might sound easy to say "go out and find your mentor", but in fact, it can be hard to think about who is the right mentor for you! Remember, you don't necessarily need to have only one mentor. It depends on your goals, and it depends on what you seek to accomplish. But remember, "Go All In" finding someone who can help you get to your goals because at the end of it all, you are supposed to get there and your mentor is supposed to get you there a lot faster.

One of my favorite lessons I still love to share with my students is about the meaning of the word "GURU." The word "Gu" means "remover" and "Ru" means "darkness." When you don't know something, when you don't know which route to go; you are in darkness and you can't see your path clearly. The mentor or guru is the one who can clear the way and lead you to the light.

I've had so many "Ah-ha!" moments while learning and working with my mentor. It is the combination of two people working in unison that makes it a complete process. Both sides work together: teacher and student — your mentor and yourself.

So many people aim to learn by going to seminar after seminar, and reading tons of books. They set tons of goals, but never end up taking action. Why? Because taking action is harder! That is why it's so important to have a mentor. You need to have consistent accountability along the way as you implement a clear plan of action. If you are really serious about getting what you want, you can't have it without taking action. Take action today and reach out to a mentor!

After you find the right person to mentor you, you need to work hard and be very coachable as well. When I found my mentor and joined her coaching program, I was so scared because the coaching program wasn't cheap and I only had eight weeks to learn and be in this intense boot camp. It also wasn't a one-on-one coaching program. It was a program with an assembly of about a hundred women who wanted to become successful entrepreneurs. I was just one of many people who were new in the entrepreneurial world. However, I worked very hard, and I was very coachable. I wanted to learn as much as I could; and most importantly, I took massive action from what I learned.

Looking back, I never regretted hiring a mentor. I never regretted the money I invested in a mentor because it has changed my business and my lifestyle so much. I now have the freedom to manage my own time, make money even when I'm not on the clock, and be around my children more. I am a much happier person because I get to wake up every day with a full purpose!

When you start something new, set some new goals, and get ready to move on to the next level of success, you will face fear and it can be a real deal-breaker. Fear makes so many people quit their dreams because changing patterns and habits takes courage that can't be dealt with on your own. You shouldn't be dealing with it on your own. That is what a mentor is for! Of course it won't be for free and will cost a lot of money but it is an investment you'll benefit from your whole life long. You will realize later on that your life is never going to be the same because you have made that commitment to go all in.

SECTION FOUR
Go All In and Overcommit

"Without a sense of urgency, desire loses its value."

—Jim Rohn

Success requires making a plan and taking massive action. When you go all in, you throw away all the excuses and are NOT allowed to tell yourself "I can't!"

Some people around you will start telling you that your dream is too big, too hard, too soon, too much, too long, too expensive, etc. Aren't you tired of that? I am! So do you need to listen to them? Absolutely not. Those who have never done big things will most likely think if they can't do it, you will never be able to either. However, people who have done great things and achieved success will say, "Go for it!", because they know that following your dreams and passion is what makes us feel alive.

Tell yourself this everyday. "Success is not something that happens to you, it's something that happens because of you." The journey isn't going to be easy anyway. The goal is supposed to be a challenge you must overcome, no matter what, so why listen to those who never dared to do it?

Many people say that "life is like a game". If you agree, then you need to be the one dictating the rules and changing this game. It's okay to be born poor — to be from a lower class family. But in my opinion, it is not okay to die poor. I was born in that poor, lower class family; but I am working hard everyday to change my game — my life — right now to create a new and better future for myself by going all in and over committing to achieving my goals.

The key to "Going All In"? Commitment and hard work. How can you be the game changer? Take action after deciding to go all in.

"Goals without taking action are only dreams."

You must also remember to think beyond what common sense would allow. Most people think that they only need to work hard, and they will succeed. Success happens when we implement good thinking, planning and work habits. Working harder means working smarter, not working for longer hours. This means thinking calmly and clearly, planning, and then working hard to achieve it.

Most people don't get this far. They may think about a lot of things, and have brilliant ideas they would be well advised to explore, but the majority of people will stop right there and just keep thinking about it.

That's what 80% of people do — they dream! Because it is easier to talk about it and pray about it than it is to get up and do it.

When you really want to achieve your dream, you can't settle for taking action only half way. You must do everything you can to get to where you want to go. You look for the opportunity or you create an opportunity for yourself. You get uncomfortable and take risks. You trust yourself and the power of the unseen forces. You act and do things as if you have already accomplished your goal. It is more powerful to go all in — to do it full-out — and take that crystal clear idea you have and transform it into reality by taking massive action.

I admire Brendon Burchard very much. In his book, *High Performance Habits*, he talks about how high performers must have something more than just passion if they want to achieve their goals. Passion is something everyone can understand. Passion is the expectation that you can stay highly emotionally engaged and laser-focused over the long-term, even when others are criticizing you. But it's also important to keep your focus and your faith. When you doubt yourself and start to wonder if they might be right and think that you don't have what it takes, you just need to stay focused on believing in yourself and believing in the good that you are doing.

The fear that comes up is your belief that something is bad. So even when you fall again and again; even when you are forced to stretch well beyond your comfort zone; even when the rewards and recognition come too far apart; even when everyone else would have given up; even when all signs say you should quit, you still need to keep going.

We can't control what other people are saying or doing. All we can do is stay focused.

"I will persist. I will win."

I promise you, if you commit to staying focused now and taking all in action, you will win someday.

Success requires a process. Show up until you make it.

10.
Overcoming Time Wasters

"Procrastination is the thief of time."

—Edward Young

When I decided to invest in myself, I ended up loving myself even more. I always knew that I was a dreamer. I love to imagine and dream very big. I also always knew that I am very capable and not afraid of hard work. I always have some extra energy left, even when working all day. I now have a hard time — and get frustrated sometimes — during the holiday when I don't get to do much. Nowadays when families get together, what do most people do? They talk, eat, watch TV and spend time on their cell phones. That makes me so frustrated because I could be doing something much better with my time and energy than just sitting in front of the TV or on the phone. I'm pretty sure that many families have the TV on at the same time that everyone is on their phones, checking Facebook and social media statuses.

WHY are we wasting our time doing things that don't matter very much? Isn't this an addiction already? It isn't a good example for the kids either. All of these feelings happened because I decided to go all in for my life and my career. My life's goal is to live fully; to be effective every day. The last thing I want to do is waste my time doing meaningless things. When you are wasting your time wandering around, spending time on something that is not productive and not really adding anything positive to your day, you've already lost. That is a life lesson.

Jim Rohn, the legendary American entrepreneur said, "If you don't decide your own life plan, chances are you will fail into someone else's plan. Guess what they may have planned for you? Not much."

Most people allow their lives to simply happen to them. They float along. They wait. They react. By the time a large portion of their life is behind them, they realize they should have been more proactive and strategic.

I hope that hasn't been true for you. If it has, then I want to encourage you to develop a stronger sense of urgency and start your day productive and meaningful.

The most common time-waster is procrastination. We're all learning to adapt to a challenging situation with all that's been happening in the world recently. Many people have to change the way they work and people have responded to the challenge in different ways. Procrastination is a challenge at the best of times and right now, as you're reading this book, it can be particularly difficult to get ourselves to sit down, focus, and work steadily. Here is how to overcome time wasters and easily beat the procrastination habit using these 3 things.

1. Set Your Schedule and Deadline

Deadlines are easy to hate but they are extremely important. Only 8% of people achieve their goals and get their work done when they set a deadline. However, organizing your time and setting deadlines means having clear prioritized to-do lists, schedules, and time frames for completing a task. Deadlines help counter procrastination when working on your goal. Without a sense of urgency, desires lose their value.

2. Limit Your Screen Time

With the coronavirus pandemic forcing people to stay at home as movie theaters close, and restaurants become unavailable for dine-ins, Americans have been spending more of their lives online. The Harris Poll found that between 46% and 51% of US adults were using social media more since the outbreak began — that translates to almost 12 new users every second.

Consider refraining from checking social media or your emails until you've accomplished at least one task from your to-do list. There are some Chrome extensions like StayFocusd and Work Mode that can block social media access while working from your desktop that can make it easier to follow through with this.

3. Find Accountability Partners

Having a good accountability partner can help you make serious progress toward any of your goals. When you fully commit to having responsibility in any process, you should find an accountability partner who can provide the inspiration, knowledge, perspective, wisdom, and feedback you need to keep you on track.

Exercise:

- Set priorities regarding what you want to achieve, plan your schedule, and then set deadlines. Be honest and kind to yourself. You shouldn't have to feel reluctant to complete your deadlines. Rather, you should have a mindset where you want to meet your deadlines because you have important reasons to do so. You'll find that it is more enjoyable that way. However, remember, if you want to have different results, you need to take a new action that you have never done before. Get excited and ready for it. After you know your goals, find someone who can hold you accountable, and keep you on track. Enjoy the process!

11.
Expand. Never Contract

If not now, when?

As I am writing this book, our world is facing a serious economic crisis. 2020 was the year that many of us had thought would be the best year. But when the coronavirus hit, and the pandemic snowballed its way across the world, what can we do? It is not only a great depression but a worldwide major economic contraction.

Most people started having the mindset of being careful and staying cautious. It sounded like the right thing to do, given the circumstances, but this self-preservation thinking is the very thing that will guarantee you that you will never get what you want. If you are facing a hard time getting results, the easiest way to solve this problem is to do things differently. "Expand rather than contract." If you aren't getting to where you want to go, stop, and look at your daily behavior.

What you are doing isn't getting you there?

Ask yourself, "What should I be doing?"; "What different actions do I need to do?"; and "How can I expand?"

A few examples:

- If you want to get in shape, will you put your focus on consistent exercise and eating habits?
- If you want a better job and make more money, will you take action to improve your skills and apply for new opportunities?
- If you want to grow and have a successful and profitable business, will you work on your business TODAY?

Because contracting is a form of retreating, it is against the concept of "Go All In." Going all in demands that you continue to act, produce, and create massive actions regardless of the situation or circumstances.

I admit that it can be difficult and counterintuitive to expand while others are taking protective actions; however, if you take advantage of the opportunity of what is happening in our world and take massive action, you will succeed. My favorite mantra that I tell myself every day is, "I will persist. I will win."

For me, 2020 has been the year of new opportunities. Many doors have opened to me. Because my yoga retreat business had to pause due to the world pandemic, I started to pivot my ideas and take massive actions towards those right away.

It wasn't an easy decision to expand. I also experienced fear once more, but I chose to push past it.I chose to expand my business rather than stop. So far, I have published my second book. I have become a best-selling author. I've been seen on TV where my message was shared to millions of people. I've also begun hosting and coaching for my dream project for passionate entrepreneurs around the country. I'm sure that there are many more opportunities lined up in the future as well.

I am so thankful that despite what is happening in our world, there can still be wins and successes for all of us. While the rest of the world withdraws, we should expand on every front possible. The first action of expanding and not contracting is getting off the sofa and making your way to your goals. Seek out opportunities and show that you are advancing in what you want to achieve.

Exercise:

Brainstorm your ideas and write it down in your journal/notebook.

What are some ways you can expand that only require creativity and energy and not money?

"I am available to more good than I have ever experienced, imagined, or realized before in my life."

—Michael Beckwith

12.
Getting Started With Go All In

You can't go back and change the beginning, but you can start where you are and change the ending.

So when should you start? The answer is most definitely, NOW.

When you learn something new, you get excited and inspired by the novel ideas and possibilities. However, if you wait even just a little bit before acting, chances are you won't do it at all. This is because procrastination will set in. If you are inspired to do something, take action right away. Otherwise, you will get sidetracked. You'll check a message on your phone, lose a few minutes, and before you know it — your kids are already awake and need breakfast, and you've already lost your momentum. Distractions lead to procrastination and that is our enemy.

If you want to improve your diet by eating lean and green, don't just think and talk about it. Think about what you will do to start now. Don't wait for the "perfect timing" to make everything unfold for you — it will never happen that way. Don't wait and take your first step.

The first step is the hardest. It is human nature to want to stay within our comfort zone. We have been trained for a long time to protect ourselves and not take risks. Ever since we were young, we have been taught not to take risks, not to run too fast, and not to do things that are too hard. Our minds were programmed to think that way for a long time such that we must fight to go against our base instincts.

Every time you want to get new results, you need to start taking different actions and start right away. If you don't and procrastinate, you won't see the results you want. Most people end up thinking that they should wait until they have more money in order to start a business. They think they should wait until they have more time to start exercising. They think they should wait until their kids grow up and leave the house to follow their passion. However, those things won't happen if you wait. Remember, there are only two times that exist for successful people — the present and the future.

Focusing your energy on the present — while keeping part of your attention on the future you're creating — is the best way to meet new goals. You certainly can't start yesterday, because it has already passed; and you can't start tomorrow, because it has yet to come. If you wait until tomorrow, you most likely will never start. There will be something else to distract you tomorrow and you would have once again postponed your future. Chances are you won't take action tomorrow if you aren't doing something to start today — so start building your future now.

Taking the first action step is not going to be a comfortable decision that gives you a cozy feeling. If you dare wait until you feel ready physically, mentally, emotionally, and financially, you'll never start. It has never worked like that for anyone ever. That magical moment of feeling completely ready will never come.

Don't wait. Don't procrastinate. Act now and keep learning and acquiring more knowledge as you go. This is how to create the future you want.

This book isn't just a conversation about success or what to do with it once you achieve it. There are hundreds of self-help books that talk about this. I'm sure you've read some that give you *5 steps to do X* or *10 ways to achieve Y.*

What I am sharing with you is more direct and simple because I know how easy it is to get lost in the details and stay stuck.

Other motivational books and programs start you off with energy and focus, but after the initial excitement, you probably found that you lost that focus quickly. I see it all the time when my clients first come to me. They have strong intentions but they fizzle out easily.

That was me for years! I would read the book, do the course, listen to the video, and be so focused for a while. But just as suddenly; I would lose my momentum, my courage, and my certainty. My journey took me to this place over and over again, but I never let go of my big vision and my big WHY. I walked — sometimes so slowly, I felt like I was walking with my knees — toward my goal and never stopped. Step by step, things have shifted.

I have now grown. I'm now meeting with Forbes, Fox News, and CNN producers. I'm still scared and often feel like I'm not quite ready to jump to the next level. I'll admit that I wanted to run away before I met with Forbes because I was so intimidated. I felt like a fraud. I said to myself that I wasn't big enough yet to be working with Forbes. But I was big enough and I'm even bigger now after that initial meeting. Some days it feels like it's happening too fast. Other days, I doubt because it seems too slow. This is all part of the journey. The trick is to start taking action right away and never give up.

Getting into the momentum is the hardest action step to take. We are moving from the stickiest place in the status quo to a whole new place we've only been dreaming about and have little experience with.

It's easy to imagine going from being overweight to being fit and slender once you lose 70 pounds. But to get out the door and go for a walk right away — to choose to purchase healthier foods at the market today — is the hard part. But once you start, you'll notice subtle shifts occurring. You'll have more energy, deeper breaths, and more stamina. You'll notice that you're losing weight, feeling better, and enjoying exercising. The morning bike rides are so much fun that you look forward to them.

That is why you can read multiple 500-page books on this and still not see any results. Taking action is the new habit you have to cultivate. If you don't, the thinking will turn into daydreaming and that is all it will be.

It will be fun and easy to just keep on daydreaming. It will feel sexy to talk about your dream house, dream body, dream marriage, dream vacation, and dream family. However, working to actually get it takes action — consistent action — and that part's not sexy. Going to bed at 2 a.m. because you're writing an article for Forbes and getting up at 6:30 a.m. for the meeting you committed to weeks ago is NOT sexy, but it does produce fabulous results. Results are sexy.

Balance is important too. I know that the work I do makes it seem like I'm a workaholic, but I'm not because I enjoy it and don't feel compelled to do it. It is fun to build my dream and see my dream come to life. I am on the other side of success now and I can say that every action step I took, every late night, every early morning, every extra effort was worth it. And if I have to do it over again for my future goals? It will still be worth it.

Whenever I get messages every day from different people, thanking me for sharing my message and helping them go after their dreams, it always invigorates me. My true story and my sincere message has impacted thousands of people and moved them to achieve their big goals — now THAT is sexy.

You have to go all in — not just make vision boards. My vision boards have been tossed into the garage. When I made them, I was like an excited kid with a new toy; but a few days later I lost all that energy. I've written in dozens of journals, but I didn't do the work. I didn't commit 100% to go all in and achieve those goals.

I was interested in these goals, but I wasn't committed to them. I wasn't committed to working hard and doing whatever it took to reach my goals. If you're just interested, you will dream and talk about it, but you won't necessarily take the action to achieve it. When you commit, you will do whatever it takes to get to your goals.

That's all you have to do to be successful. This is the formula.
Go all in and commit to your goals and you'll reach them.

Do not overthink it. Keep it simple and straightforward. A lot of people think about what is impossible way more than they think about what is possible. We want to avoid failure so badly, we think of all the things that can go wrong. We overthink ourselves out of our dreams. We always conclude that we don't know how to reach our goal.

There is a missing link and it confuses and worries us. Of course you wouldn't know how to do it. If you did then you would already have it. The excuses of not having enough money, or training, or connections; excuses of being too old or too young to start; the list of reasons to NOT to do it never ends. Once you get over that, your desire and goal will be on the horizon. So you need a new way of showing up.

Make it simple. Make a commitment. Take action. Find a mentor and get help and guidance to get through the challenges you face.

You may start off wanting to write a book or run a marathon, but there will be even bigger goals you will want after that which will require even more action and focus than your previous goal. It never ends. That is why you have to cultivate the new habit of committing. It will keep you on track when you learn how to take action without overthinking.

As you get started on this journey of going all in, you may feel a bit overwhelmed. You might notice that friends and family and others around you start to tell you, "It's too much." They will suggest that you set a "realistic goal." They'll tell you to "Be careful."; "Play it safe."; and that "Money won't make you happy." Don't be tempted to wait, slow down or overthink!

Do not downsize your goals as you are working toward them. Stay focused! Do not get lost in the details of how you will achieve them but ask yourself, "What actions can I take today to move me toward my goals?" Do whatever it takes regardless of what they are and how you feel.

You're like a car in the mud. You just need enough traction to move an inch, and then you can begin to get out. The journey might seem dirty, but it's certainly better than being stuck.

Getting started with the "Go All In" formula will help you create a strong mental framework every day. It's just like exercising to gain strong muscles for your body. You need to "innercise" (inner + exercise = innercise) to get your mind strong as well. So when people give you negative advice, tell them that you would rather commit to your goals and that even if you fail you won't be disappointed. Tell them that you would regret it more for never trying.

Your success probably won't happen overnight, but that shouldn't stop you from continuing. You need to stay in your lane, break old habits that held you back, and go all the way in with your plans.

When I decided to share my message with more people, I learned how to prepare my pitch to TV stations and other media networks. I was afraid they would reject me or tell me that my message wasn't good enough. I was always wondering if they would be interested in what I had to share. Was I smart enough? The list of doubts went on and on, but I did it anyway.

I was sending out a lot of emails to different TV producers and pitching them my ideas. The next morning, I took another scary massive action by calling the newsdesk and asking to connect directly with their producer. Once I got her information, I sent out another email to her. I let go of whatever I was feeling and thinking after that. I did everything I could, so I relaxed and let it go.

A few hours later, the producer replied to me and said she loved my ideas and wanted to know if I was available to be on their show next Monday. I replied to her right away saying, "YES, I am available."

Was I ready for a live interview? No, but I said "yes" anyway. The next day, the same producer emailed me again and asked if they could interview me twice on that day because they really liked my ideas and what I had to offer.

What did I say? Of course, I said, "YES!"

Was I ready for two interview segments? No. Did I know what they would ask me? No. Did I prepare for my interview as best I can? Yes! So that day, I was on a TV twice and everything went well.

Go All In.

Do whatever it takes to get closer to your goals every day.

Don't wait. Start now. Show up 101%.

Continue to add wood to the things you could control. Every time you experience a setback and disappointment, go back to read your goals. This will help you remain focused on your destination instead of difficulties. It creates a type of force inside of you that connects you with your goal. Keep your eyes on your target no matter what, keep fueling the fire. Commit to "Go All In" thinking and "Go All In" action.

This is the major difference between people who achieve their goals and people who don't. Because if you don't go all in, nothing else matters. Make your goals so big that others will have no choice but to sit around and watch you succeed.

Remember, you will never be ready and you will never have all the answers. There won't be any "perfect timings" nor "green lights" on when to start. There will always be obstacles and difficulties when you start and more will appear as you go. However, keep taking action, go all in consistently, and persistently.

Follow through on your responsibility to leave a legacy and your footprint on this planet.

Give Yourself a Chance to Go All In = Give Yourself a Chance to Win

—Nim Stant

About the Author

Nim Stant, Success Mentor, Yoga Professional, Motivational Speaker, Founder and CEO of Go All In TV and Host of Go All In Podcast.

Coming from the third world country of Thailand and growing up in a middle-class family has taught her to become a purpose-driven entrepreneur who always seeks to live to the fullest potential. Nim created innovative strategies to dramatically amplify her personal and professional performance.

With 20 years of experience, Nim has now dedicated her life to inspire others to let go of their limiting beliefs, commit to their dreams and goals, and take real action. In her book, Go All In, Nim reveals the principles of Go All In to empower others to practice and step up toward lifelong results.

Nim also hosts countless yoga and healing retreats across the world. She has been featured in 3TV, The Health Journal, Fitness Republic, and was interviewed by Kajabi — one of the most sophisticated solutions on the market for creating online course platforms. She has inspired over 47,000 entrepreneurs to reinvent their businesses during the global crisis.

Made in the USA
Middletown, DE
24 October 2022